T0160896

POSSIBILITIES

POEMS OF
LIFE AND LOVE

KATHRYN CAROLE ELLISON

Published by Lady Bug Books, an imprint of Brisance Books Group.
Lady Bug Press and the distinctive ladybug logo are registered trademarks of
Lady Bug Books, LLC.

Lady Bug Books
400 112th Avenue N.E.
Suite 230
Bellevue, WA 98004
www.GiftsOfLove.com

For information about custom editions, special sales and permissions, please email
Info@GiftsOfLove.com

Manufactured in the United States of America
ISBN: 978-1-944194-81-9

First Edition: June 2021

A NOTE FROM THE AUTHOR

The poems in this book were written over many years as gifts to my children. I began writing them in the 1970s, when they were reaching the age of reason. And, as I found myself in the position of becoming a single parent, I wanted to do something special to share with them – something that would become a tradition, a ritual they could count on.

And so the Advent Poems began – one day, decades ago – with a poem 'gifted' to them each day during the Advent period leading up to Christmas, December 1 to December 24. Forty some years later... my children still look forward each year to the poems that started a family tradition, that new generations have come to cherish.

It is my sincere hope that you will embrace and enjoy them, and share them with those you love.

Children of the Light was among the early poems I wrote, and is included in each of the *Poems of Life and Love* books in The Ellison Collection: *Heartstrings, Celebrations, Inspirations, Sanctuary, Awakenings, Sojourns, Milestones, Tapestry, Gratitude, Beginnings, Horizons, Moments, Possibilities, Mindfulness and Reflections*. After writing many hundreds of poems, it is still my favorite. The words came from my heart... and my soul... and flowed so effortlessly that it was written in a single sitting.
All I needed to do was capture the words on paper.

Light, to me, represented all that was good and pure and right with the world, and I believed then – as I do today – that those elements live in my children, and perhaps in all of us. We need only to dare.

– KCE

DEDICATION

To my parents: Herb and Bernice Haas

Mom, you were the poet who went before me...
unpublished, but appreciated nonetheless.

And Dad, you always believed in me,
no matter what direction my life took.
Thank you for your faith in me,
and for your unconditional love.

TABLE OF CONTENTS

LIFE'S JOYS

LIFE'S LESSONS

LIFE'S GIFTS

LIFE'S JOYS

POSSIBILITIES... WHAT IF?

The mind is an amazing, wonderful thing!
What people can think about can be most exciting...
Or not... it depends on what their hearts can hold.
Is it warmth and kindness, or bitter cold?

I choose to ponder the warmer, kinder heart
Which shows compassion and practices the art
Of working together with others for the benefit
Of an all-inclusive world... a dream, I admit.

It's the possibility of having a dream come true
That makes life interesting... and to continue –
When nothing is sure, everything is possible.
Every day holds the possibility of a miracle!

A Buddhist monk, by the name Thich Nhat Hanh,
Wrote about possibility – his words a voice of reason.
Clear and concise, the meaning quite intelligible:
"Because you are alive, everything is possible."

What if a transformation could take place?
What if... instead of confrontation face to face
Between two camps so divisive and stubborn...
They could come together and cooperatively govern?

What if... people wanted to take care of each other,
Coming together for common good, sister and brother?
What if... our beautiful planet could thrive,
And each and everyone of us could feel more alive?

What if... our air could be breathable again,
And our fish in the oceans, in good health, could swim?
What if... all of us experienced good health?
What if friendship and cooperation were measures of wealth?

So many things are possible when we think they are!
Our possibilities are endless; imagination will take us far!
With possibilities, we begin each new day.
Let's get started on the possibilities straightaway!

ANTICIPATION

The difference between anticipation and anxiety
Is simply the flipping of a switch.
Depending upon your basic approach to life
You'll soon know which rules, without a hitch.

Anticipation is an important part of life
Because it is born of hope.
Anticipation lets you know you are truly alive!
Conversely, with anxiety you feel like a dope!

Wisdom consists of anticipating the consequences
Of your actions, your words and your thoughts.
Like it or not, you are totally responsible
For a life well-lived, or one tied in knots.

There are far, far better things ahead
Than any you leave behind.
Anticipating them makes pleasure more intense.
Flip the switch to anticipation in your mind.

PROSPERITY

Make time for singing, for dancing and play time, as well;
Because, if you're wise,
Your spirit will rise;
In all of your fields you'll excel.

It's a grand time for living; it's a time for family and friends.
No matter how much
Possession you touch,
Your spirit wealth always transcends.

Do what you love in life, and success will be coming to you;
So live for today
In your own special way.
Be happy in all that you do.

REBIRTH

"I've lost touch with a couple of people I used to be!"
I attribute these clever words to Joan Didion.
Like Joan, we all undergo changes in our lives...
Almost always for the better, in the long run.

Spring is the time of the year when Rebirth
Cannot be avoided – it's all around to be seen.
Blossom by blossom, Spring begins each year.
Nature is bent on new beginnings, it would seem.

Rebirth cannot come without change, without death.
Last season's leaves become mulch for new fruit.
Spring is our reminder of how beautiful change can be.
It is the land reawakening with each new shoot.

We're in a perpetual renewal of birth and growth.
Every moment we are dying and being reborn.
Spring breathes new life into the world around us.
When change occurs, oh please do not mourn.

How do you plan for your rebirth to happen?
Your game begins anew. You decide when.
Be free of limitations; be reborn and take flight.
Don't ever be afraid to start over again.

CHILDREN OF THE LIGHT

There are those souls who bring the light,
Who spill it out for all to share.
And with a joy that does excite,
They show the world that they do care.
It is so very bright.

In this sharing, love does pervade
Into their lives and cycles round;
And as this light is outward played
The love is also inward bound.
It is an awesome trade.

You are a soul whose light is shared.
It comes from deep within your heart.
It's best because it is not spared,
Because it's total, not just part.
And I am glad you've dared.

THE BIRTHRIGHT

Ownership of who you are and of what you do
Is a birthright that is yours and yours alone;
With it a guarantee that is carved in stone...
The right to live your life you can pursue.

Each one of us holds power that's within
To become who we wish in thought and deed.
To find it is a joy, it is agreed.
The birthright all along has been built in.

Resolve to find yourself by taking hold
Of the birthright that lives within us all.
And hear the misery thunder in its fall,
As you progress on line with movement bold.

DREAMS

Some people give up; they're hung up on "age,"
And pursue life with a little less steam.
You are never too old to set another goal
Or to dream another new dream.

A dream is never a waste of one's life...
Dreams are realities in waiting!
In dreams we plant the seeds of our future.
The joy is in the anticipating.

Never give up on a dream just because
Of the time it will take to accomplish.
The time will pass anyway, like it or not.
Your reasoning to give up is just gibberish.

Never let the thought of failure stop you
On your path to reaching your dream.
Positive thinking, keeping the end in mind,
Is the key to success, it would seem.

The goal is to die with memories, not dreams;
Pursue your dreams as far as you must.
Do everything possible to make them come true.
Your happiness depends on it, I trust.

GET BUSY ON THE POSSIBLE

Some people sit home and dream of success,
While others go out and make it happen.
There's a lesson there, and it's not very subtle.
Everything you want requires some action.

It's said that if you want to accomplish the impossible,
There's really only one place to begin.
Think it is possible, and make it happen.
Then the "impossible" is not. Success you will win.

Being afraid of what could go wrong
And then staying home afraid to try
Will not get you anywhere (believe me on this)
Except, perhaps, staying home to cry.

Don't get discouraged, and don't lose faith
In yourself and in what you want to do.
Keep busy, and always be optimistic.
You'll succeed before you're through.

CREATOR

You create your own reality... it's true!
And it depends on your inner strength.
To make your world the heaven it is
You must be willing to go the extra length.

We are all an actual part of God.
We carry in our soul a spark of the Divine.
This spark can be used to do great things...
To make our world better, by design.

The most pressing need is to remold the world,
Removing the negative by crowding it out.
From your God-Center within, release the spark
And create your heaven as you walk about.

Allow the goodness and beauty within
To create that heaven on earth around you.
Control the negativity that tries to creep in.
Do not let it pervade all you view.

FOOD

Eat to nourish your body
Rather than simply for joy.
Be conscious of every bite you take;
Discipline you must employ.

Chew every bite very carefully,
Drawing energy from every mouthful.
Imagine that energy as it reaches
From your toes up to your skull.

Eat carefully and avoid eating food
If you are upset or are feeling sick;
Your mood when you take food in
Will make it taste good or sink like a brick!

Eat food of different colors
To put your diet in balance.
A red, a yellow, a green, a brown –
Combine with your own best talents.

Eat light foods to offset the heavy.
Don't make too much of a good thing!
And be sure to drink lots of liquid –
Water's best – you could buy a spring!

And exercise – oh yes, don't forget –
Do something for your body each day.
And as you move, be conscious of
Your life force as cells interplay.

LOVE

It's easy to believe there's only one kind of love,
But in reading, you'll find there are many;
All named by the Greeks, their subtleties explained,
And repeated... repeated in litany.

The many types all are based on just one;
Love doesn't exist in a plurality.
The various descriptions are just manifestations
Of love, a single reality.

To lose yourself in another's arms
Or in another's company;
Or to lose yourself in suffering for
All victims, and there are many.

To lose yourself in any of the ways,
Some of which are described above,
Is the only way to find yourself.
And the word for it is "love."

Of all the powers, love carries the most clout;
It has no counterpart.
Love alone can conquer the final bastion.
It can win the human heart.

But also it can be as powerless as a kitten.
By itself it remains impotent.
It needs direction and gentle prodding.
It can do nothing except by consent.

FAITH

Faith is a tool, like any other,
But there's one very important exception.
Because of your connection to the All That Is,
Your faith takes on a more powerful conception.

When the world seems darkest – you're struggling to survive –
Your faith can get you over the worst.
To apply your faith in times of need
Look to God, but trust your own strength first.

If your strength fails you, as it well might,
Then have enough faith to ask for aid
From your God who's always with you.
Know that the love connection will never fade.

You are never asked to endure any more
Than your soul can take, so it's said.
Every prayer is answered; rely on that knowledge.
You will continue through life undefeated.

FOR ALL WE DO

Doing for the sake of doing,
To contribute to a bigger picture,
Is reward enough at the end of the day;
You've left your mark, your "tincture."

What you do will have (or maybe it won't)
A significant impact on the outcome.
It will make a difference (or maybe not).
To not need recognition shows wisdom.

All you need do is ACT (the key word)
To begin the process at hand,
Then watch what happens; you'll be amazed!
The outcome can potentially be grand.

But if it's not, as may be the case,
You've acted. You've gotten it going.
You have contributed your talent to the cause,
And your reward is in the doing.

YOU ALWAYS HAVE A CHANCE

Within you at this moment is all the power
To do things you never thought possible!
If you did all the things you're capable of doing
Your astonishment would be incredible!

This power will become available to you
The moment your beliefs change from "can't" to "can."
You can do anything at all that you wish to do.
You're limited only by self-doubt, you understand.

You know what you are today, but not
What you may be tomorrow.
Always look at things as they can be,
And lose the feeling of sorrow.

Life's lessons

RESPONSIBILITY

The most important letter in the word
"Responsibility" is "I." It is true!
When a job needs doing, it's easy to look away,
But instead, say, "I'll be the one to do."

Being able to see what should be done
Is a sign you're big enough to do it.
Take the initiative; you'll be glad you did.
And once started on the job, don't quit.

People flock to winners. It's true, you know,
Leaving losers in the quagmire.
Doers attract like people to them.
Doers do indeed inspire.

Vision... Action... Accomplishment!
Fortune's pattern is outlined for you.
See a thing, then go after it with vigor.
You'll succeed because you believe in you.

You cheat yourself if you leave it to others.
You lose out on the joy of the chase.
And when you've finished the job at hand,
You can walk away in grace.

Responsibility is like anything else...
Once you own it, it is yours forever
To do with whatever you choose to do.
It's an amazingly powerful lever.

NEVER GIVE UP!

And so the quest continues... it does...
The quest to find your way.
You're incredibly strong, and capable of
Making whatever you choose really pay!

Payment comes to you in may forms –
A living wage with a margin for fun,
And the joy you feel in being of service,
A feeling of self-worth that makes you Number One!

Whatever you choose you'll reach as high
As you want to, and that's a fact.
Use your heads, your hearts and your bodies, too,
And with yourself make a pact
To never give up, no matter what.
You have what it takes, no doubt.
If someone tries to get in your way,
Just give them a sample of your 'clout.'

THE ULTIMATE AIM

"The ultimate aim of all humans: to obtain
Happiness and a sense of fulfillment."
The Dalai Lama's words give form
To the concept of enlightenment.
The feeling you have as you end each day
Is a simple form of measurement
Of how close you are to reach your intent
Of having joy and having accomplishment.
Combining both mental and material approach,
Not choosing one single element
Is important, he says, to achieving your goal.
The two methods really do complement.

OVERCOMING A BURDEN

When I was just a little girl
My Momma said something to me.
It has served me well through thick and thin.
It will serve you, too – I guarantee.

The words she uttered have been carried by me
For many, many years.
About the time I'm ready to pack it in,
And find myself in tears,
I remember them and then I smile;
For they've been ever true.
And so today seems an appropriate time
To pass them on to you.

She said, "The good Lord never gave me a load
That together He and I can't carry."
And when times get rough and I think "I can't,"
Their memory dissolves the fear. I'm no longer wary.

Fear is the single most negative thing
To overcome in our daily humdrum.
It's insidious, it creeps right in,
But love always will overcome.

OPPORTUNITIES

The greatest of all the martial arts are those
Which allow the aggressor the opportunity to fall.
They are the gentlest, the ones which require little;
Where timing and balance win over all.

True, too, the most famous of generals are those
Who do not rush their troops quickly into battle.
But first they offer their enemies ample opportunities
To make a number of self-defeating errors.

Successful company heads, administrators,
Do not meet production goals by limiting staff,
But give them opportunities to blossom;
Then watch as sales go flying off the graph.

When motivating others to excel
It's best to offer opportunities.
You'll reap returns beyond your expectations,
'Cause happy fellow workers like to please.

When things in one's life happen naturally
There is no sense of undue obligation.
Life becomes an opportunity to grow,
And to rejoice with unbridled jubilation.

POSITIVE THINKING

Some people grumble that roses have thorns...
Be grateful that thorns have roses!
Attitude marks the main difference in people.
Don't be the kind who always opposes.

A positive attitude starts a chain reaction
Of positive thoughts, events and outcomes.
It's a catalyst that sparks extraordinary results.
It is a "tried and true" of all the wisdoms.

A suggested way of living is to look for the good;
Stay away from negative messengers.
Speak of others' virtues, not their faults,
And beware of unfriendly challengers.

In your personal lives, remember "thoughts become things."
Choose wisely, and opt only for the good ones.
Remember that limitations are only imaginary.
Move ahead and broaden your horizons.

You are essentially who you create yourself to be.
What occurs in your life is your own making.
Don't dwell on the past, learn and dance on.
Control of your life is yours for the taking.

"A man is a product of his habitual thoughts,
And what he thinks he becomes."
Mahatma Gandhi shared this important wisdom.
Make thinking positively one of your customs.

SURRENDER

Always say "yes" to the present moment.
It's futile to resist what already is.
It would be insane to oppose life itself,
Which is now, it's now. Now it is!

Surrender to what is; say "yes" to life,
And be amazed at the results that come next.
Life suddenly starts working for, not against, you.
Let the world embrace you, don't be perplexed.

Amazing things happen when you surrender, and simply love;
You melt into the power already within you.
The world changes when you change, and softens when you soften.
The world loves you when you decide to love it, too.

Be willing to let go of the life that you have,
So you can have the life that is waiting in the wings.
If you surrender completely to each present moment,
You'll live more richly as human beings.

UNSELFISHNESS

The magnet in your heart that attracts true friends
Is unselfishness, and thinking of the other guy...
His story, his needs, his life experiences.
Go beyond yourselves. Your blessings will multiply.

A wise unselfishness is not a surrender
Of yourself to the wishes of anyone or anything.
It is only the best discoverable course of action,
Sharing the interests of others, notwithstanding.

Write your name in sand... it will wash.
Write your name in air... it will blow.
Write your name in the hearts of people...
It will stay forever in the afterglow.

THE SECRET OF LIFE IS NO SECRET

It is said the secret of life is meaningless
Unless you're the one to discover it.
Obviously, another person's secret of life
Would, for you, be an improper fit.

Some pretty smart folks have tried to define
What the secret of life was for them.
Here are some of their thoughts for your information.
You can take it from there (with enthusiasm).

One of their secrets of life sounded simple,
Though it undoubtedly would take effort to unlock.
You are urged to change attitude and instead of giving up,
Make stepping stones out of stumbling blocks.

On the subject of attitude, be open to change.
Welcome surprise as you live life to the fullest.
You'll know the secret of creativity, as you pursue your dreams.
The secret of life is yours to find through your interest.

When you first begin fighting for your dreams
(And with little experience) you'll make mistakes.
But the secret of success, the secret of life,
Is to fall seven times, and get up eight!

The secret of life is not in what happens...
It's what you do with what happens to you.
The secret's not always to do what you like;
But, instead, to like what you do.

A SENSE OF WONDER

From birth, a child is bombarded by experiences
That instill a sense of wonder quite profound.
According to Socrates, wonder is the beginning of wisdom.
Nature is the first place a sense of wonder is found.

Dew on a spider's web; a robin building it's nest...
A dog licking an ice cream cone in the park...
Discovering the world around him, the child begins
His journey to make his own mark.

What is grand about childhood? Everything is a wonder!
It is not merely a miracle-filled world.
Oh no, quite the opposite! With wonder at every turn,
It is a miraculous world to be discovered and unfurled.

Human growth has no limits; it's boundaries are infinite!
Intelligence, imagination and wonder are the guides.
By looking at everything as if you are seeing it anew,
You'll not lose your sense of wonder. In you it resides.

People love to wonder, and that's the seed of science.
We've been to the moon and back, and then beyond!
We've improved medicine and agriculture; people live longer lives.
To the miracles in our lives we are happy to respond.

There's so much to see – there's so much to learn;
Our time here on earth is brief.
I would rather have a mind that is opened by wonder
Than one that is closed by belief!

MISTAKES ARE A SIGN OF GROWING

When you were young, say two or three
A world of risks was yours for the taking.
You approached each risk without benefit of committee,
And you worried not about mistakes you'd be making.

You got back up and tried the stunt again
And failed, or else succeeded to completion.
You didn't fuss much, you didn't complain;
Your ego didn't seem to face depletion.

The years have passed and you're now "mature."
A fear of looking foolish if you try and fail
Will prevent your growth; you'll feel insecure.
You'll be on your path of self-betrayal.

Remember, your mistakes are learning tools.
Without them there'd be little growth at all.
Be gentle with yourself; and play the fool,
And know that mistakes do not bring downfall.

WAYS TO SHOW LOVE

There are many ways to show one's love
And you seem to have the key.
Your patience and kindness and caring ways
Result in letting people be...
Just who they are, without expectations.
You don't judge their actions or deeds.
You understand quite thoroughly
That people act out of their needs.

That's why your friendship is sought by others.
You provide a loving space for them to be
Who they really are without the hassle
Of having to prove they're okay.
I applaud your abilities and learn so much
As I watch you go through your days.
And I learn most of all as you do your dance
That unconditional love pays.

BELIEVE IN ABUNDANCE

Start with big dreams and make life worth living.
Think only in terms of abundance.
Free up your imagination, and do what you love.
You'll have success in every performance.

Receiving abundance is a process of letting go
Of all the doubts and fears, I believe.
Negative thinking blocks the abundance in your life.
Stay open in order to receive.

Plant seeds of happiness, hope, success and love.
It will all come back to you in abundance.
It's the law of nature by which you must live.
Never doubt the level of its importance.

A generous heart that is filled with gratitude
Is a magnet for a life of abundance.
If you stop giving, abundance stops, too.
So love and be loved. Keep the balance.

Think in terms of abundance! Your life is a privilege.
Make positive living your life's project.
Expect success, abundance and happiness.
You will attract that which you expect.

MOVING THROUGH FEAR

Fear is something to move right through,
Not something to be turned away from.
Remember the expression, "Face your fears!"
And when you do it, you gain your freedom.

Fear tells you that you cannot succeed;
Excitement is wanting to get in the game.
The wonderful truth about all this is
The sensations inside feel just the same.

So, in this new light, fear can be seen
For what it is – in each translation.
It can provide energy to do your best
In every new configuration.

Use your fear before it gets a chance
To bruise your soul and your efforts so fine.
When "Oh, No!" pops up, just turn it around
To "Oh Yes!" Success will be your gold mine.

LIFE'S GIFTS

SHARE YOUR LIFE

Who says we don't need people around
With whom to share our way?
Only a fool, in my estimation,
Would ever refuse to play
The Game Of Life with all he meets,
And with all its ups and downs.
Sometimes it's good, and sometimes it's not;
Sometimes it's "Send In The Clowns."

But whatever it is, it's not at all dull
When you share it with people who
Will share their "Game" and all their joys
And all their sorrows with you.
It makes life great; it makes life grand;
It makes getting up early in the day
Something to look forward to, something to take joy in,
'Cause you have people to share the way.

LIVING ARTFULLY

Living artfully takes time, it's not done in a flash,
But the result is worth the extra strain.
To establish your soul's expression, it takes more than cash.
It requires patience and the use of your brain.
And you might have to sort through some trash
To find that special prize that speaks to your core
That, when viewed, says *you* as a metaphor.

Good linens, a special rug, or a lamp can be a source
Of enriching your lives and your children's, as well.
The soul basks in this extension of time, of course.
In this object it's possible for your soul to dwell.
Collecting soulful things is a practice I endorse.
Buy, find, or create a special object that won't perish
That both you and your future generations will cherish.

SELFLESSNESS

Life takes on deeper meaning when you can give
Yourself to some cause outside of your center.
You become an owner of your own life,
And no longer are just a "renter."

In pursuit of the love and conviction, you find
Peace and satisfaction galore.
Life then offers you positive choices.
Mental health improves more and more.

Days can be dull and boring to those
Who don't go "outside" for stimulation.
Having a reason to get up in the morning
Gives the heart a positive palpitation.

The animal lives on the level of survival,
Without much thought beyond just getting along.
To man there are matters more important –
Matters that bring to his heart a song.

Some find the bigger values in such areas as religion.
Others find it in love for their fellow man;
For some, loyalty to country, or righting the wrongs,
Or feeding the hungry when they can.

Whatever it is that excites you to do,
And sends your senses reeling,
Is bound to consume you; you'll not be the same
If you get out of yourself and start feeling.

INGENUITY

Ingenuity, plus courage, plus work, equals miracles...
A proven method for success in every endeavor.
Success doesn't just happen, as if by magic.
It's a product of hard work, ingenuity, and fervor.

Ingenuity gives the ability to solve difficult problems
Within an original and creative framework.
You won't change anything if you try to reproduce it.
Change requires doing something different... all hard work.

Better is possible. It does not take genius.
It takes diligence, moral clarity and ingenuity.
Above all, it takes a willingness to try,
Keeping true at all times to your own integrity.

Innovation comes out of great human ingenuity.
Add your personal passions for good measure.
When the struggle is great the level of ingenuity should be high,
As you reach for your goals in your adventure.

You must be creative as you pursue your prize.
Your possibilities, as you know, are limitless.
Necessity may be the mother of invention,
But ingenuity is the bombshell of success.

CREATE YOUR OWN MERIT

Grow up! Who cares...
What others think of you?
There's no strength in depending
On others' thoughts of you!

You have been given your own work to do.
Get to it now – don't wonder who's watching you.

Never depend on the admiration of others,
Whether brothers or sisters... fathers or mothers.

What others think of you is none of your business.
Personal merit is not derived from an external source.

What is really yours, and yours alone?
It's the use you make of what you own...
Your ideas, resources, and opportunities;
Your books, your tools, pursue with impunity.
Make the most of what's at hand, my friend.
Be happy with yourself; your joy will know no end.

YOUR MAIN TASK

Your main task in life is to give birth to yourself;
To become all you can potentially be!
The most important product of your effort
Is your own personality!!

TRAVEL AND ADVENTURE

We travel not to escape our lives, oh no,
But for life not to leave us behind.
Traveling brings us a change of place,
And imparts new vigor to the mind.

Travel is the ONLY thing you can buy
That makes you richer... that's for sure.
One's destination is never a place,
But a new way of seeing... an adventure.

Investment in travel is an investment in yourself;
You can grow beyond your perceptions.
A mind that is stretched by a new experience
Can never go back to its old dimensions

Traveling leaves you speechless, and in return,
When asked by others about your trip,
It turns you into a wonderful story teller...
The people, the places, the companionship!

One's destination is never a place,
But a way of seeing things anew.
Wherever you go, go with all your heart;
Joy in adventure you must pursue.

POWER

Acquisition of power is the opening of yourself
To all sources of power at your command.
As your powers increase by leaps and bounds
You will, more and more, understand.

With the power of **wisdom** you inherit great knowledge,
And the experience of all the ages.
You stand on the shoulders of giants. They are
A collection of all the sages.

The power of **thought** lies in your mind,
From where all great living must spring.
The quality of your thoughts is very important.
Your destiny is determined by that very thing.

The power of the **heart** makes all things possible.
Dynamic achievers have emotional drive.
'Passion' is another word for heart power.
When you have it, you know you're alive.

The power of a **dream**, when followed to its end,
Is obsession that will not be denied.
As your dream unfolds, and comes into being,
Hang on! It will be quite a ride!

The power of **people** in your life is amazing!
Character and ideals are contagious.
Being around those who aspire to the best,
You will find to be advantageous.

The power of the **spirit** is the greatest power of all.
Napoleon learned this truth the hard way.
On failing in his quest to rule the world, he said,
"The sword will lose to the spirit any day."

The power of the **Infinite** – The All That Is –
Provides you with spiritual guidance.
Listen and learn as you walk your path,
And as you dance your dance.

SMILE

Generally, we're as happy as we make up our minds to be.
Amazing is the power we hold, you and me!
We can light up someone's life with just a smile,
Which can give them the strength to go another mile.
The opposite is true, but we won't go there.
We'll stay on the high road in cooler, cleaner air.

A smile is an action of love... takes a moment.
The response is a smile, most times without comment.
A smile is the universal language of kindness.
It always gives off an aura of cheerfulness.
Everyone smiles in the same language the world over.
It's a universal language, all its own, moreover.

We'll never know how much good one smile can cause,
And if we did, it would give us pause.
We must choose joy, and choose it every day.
Joy makes every day a holiday!
A smile is all it takes to make each day better,
So share your smiles. Make someone's day a red-letter!

*A smile costs nothing
but creates much.
It happens in a flash
but the memory
can sometimes last forever.
It is something
that cannot be bought, begged,
borrowed or stolen,
For it is something that has no value
until it is given away.*

– Anonymous

PERFECTION

Perfection is a goal to hold in view,
But not too tightly, lest we ourselves undo.
We somehow think that we must always be
That little robot person, error free.

The human element works all the time,
And gives us quirks that are sublime.
They make us fun to know, though sometimes trying;
And folks who love us most sometimes are crying.

Remember, please, that humans raise and teach us,
So that other humans are able to reach us.
If it were possible to teach perfection,
We'd never grow beyond our own reflection.

A CLOSING THOUGHT

POETRY

It's the revelation
Of a sensation
That the poet
(Wouldn't you know it)
Believes to be
Felt only interiorly
And personal to
The writer who
... **writes it.**

It's the interpretation
Of a sensation
That was fueled by
A poet's sigh
And believed to be
Shared mutually
And personal to
The lucky one who
... **reads it.**

About the Author

Kathryn Carole Ellison is a former newspaper columnist
and journalist and, of course, a poet.

She lives near her children and stepchildren and their families in the
Pacific Northwest, and spends winters in the sunshine of Arizona.

You might find her on the golf course with friends, river rafting, traveling
the world, writing poems... or enjoying the Opera and the Symphony.

Late Bloomer

Our culture honors youth with all
It's unbridled effervescence.
We older ones sit back and nod
As if in acquiescence.

And when our confidence really gels
In early convalescence...
"We can't be getting old!" we cry,
"We're still struggling with adolescence!"

Acknowledgments

I have many people to thank...

First of all, my amazing children—Jon and Nicole LaFollette—for inspiring the writing of these poems in the first place. And for encouraging me to continue my writing, even though their wisdom and compassion surpass mine... and to my dear daughter-in-law and friend, Eva LaFollette, whose encouragement and interest are so appreciated.

My wonderful stepchildren, Debbie and John Bacon, Jeff and Sandy Ellison, and Tom and Sue Ellison who, with their children and grandchildren, continue to be a major part of my life; and are loved deeply by me. These poems are for you, too.

My good friends who have received a poem or two of mine in their Christmas cards these many years, for complimenting me on the messages in my poems. Your encouragement kept me writing and gave me the courage to publish.

To Kim Kiyosaki who introduced me to the right person to get the publishing process under way... Mona Gambetta with Brisance Books Group. I marvel at her experience and know-how to make these books happen.

To Amy Anderson, Sonya Kopetz, Kerri Kazarba Schneider, and Ingrid Pape-Sheldon, my very creative public relations team of experts, who have carried my story to the world.

And finally, to John B. Laughlin, a fellow traveler in life, who encourages me every day in the writing and publishing process. John, I love having you in my cheering section.

BOOKS OF LOVE
by Kathryn Carole Ellison